Are We There Yet?
All About the Planet Uranus!
Space for Kids
Children's Aeronautics & Space Book

Uranus is
the seventh
planet from
the Sun.

Uranus boasts
a majestic blue/
green haze
because of
methane gas.

Uranus is
rolling like a
barrel instead
of spinning like
the Earth and
other planets.

Uranus was
the first planet
discovered
using a
telescope.

It takes 84
Earth years
for Uranus
to go around
the sun.

Its
atmosphere
is mostly
hydrogen and
methane.

Uranus cannot
be seen by
the naked eye,
but it can be
seen using a
telescope.

In 1787, Uranus was first seen by William Herschel.

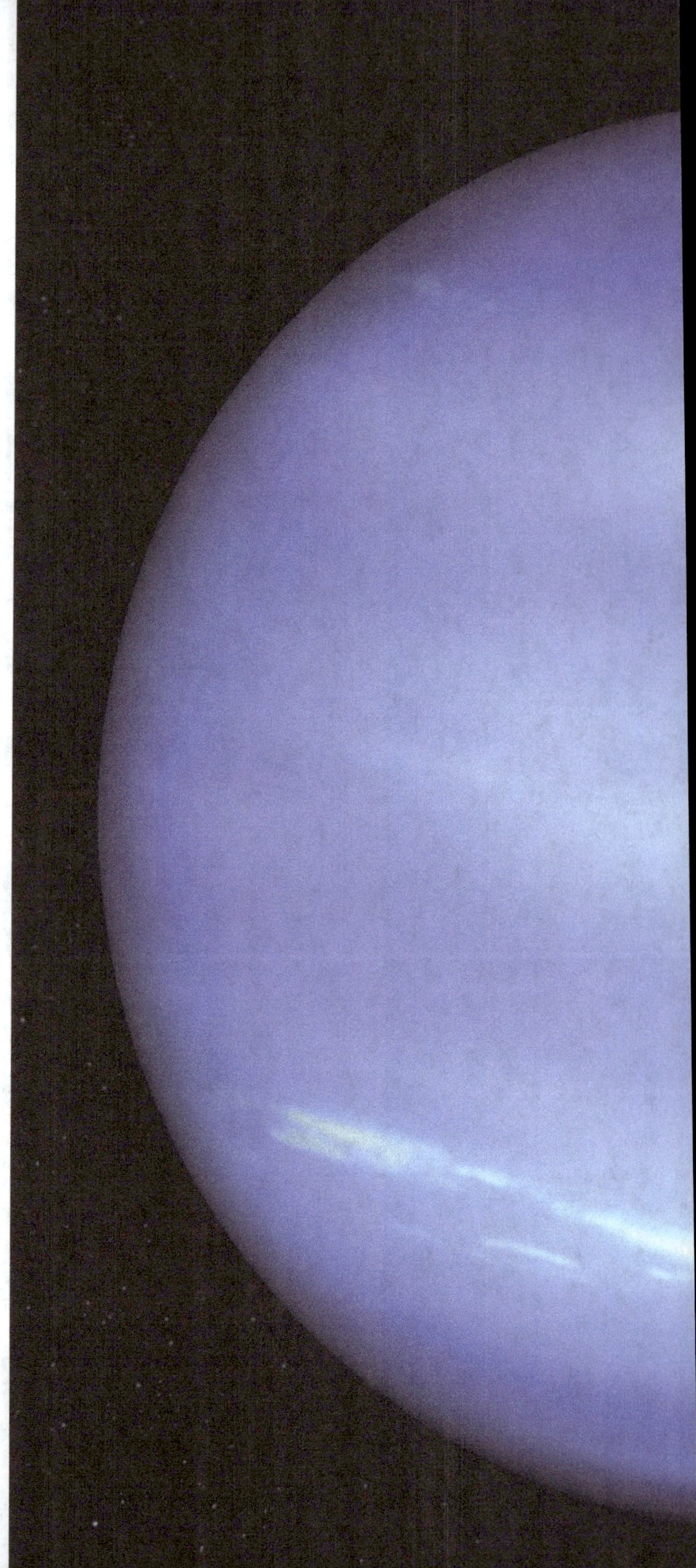

Herschel also discovered 2 of Uranus' moons.

Uranus has
a total of 27
moons.

Most of the
center of this
planet is a
frozen mass
of ammonia
and methane.

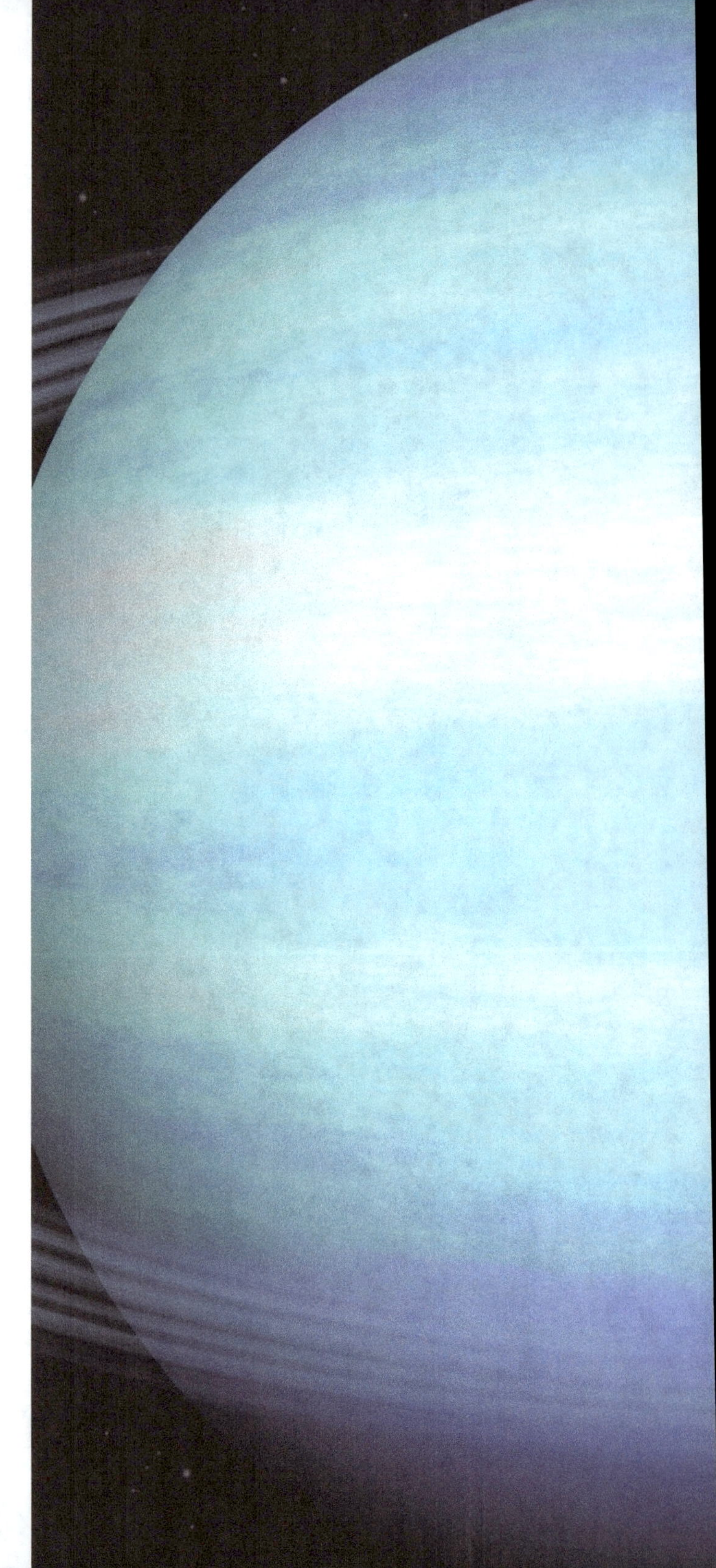

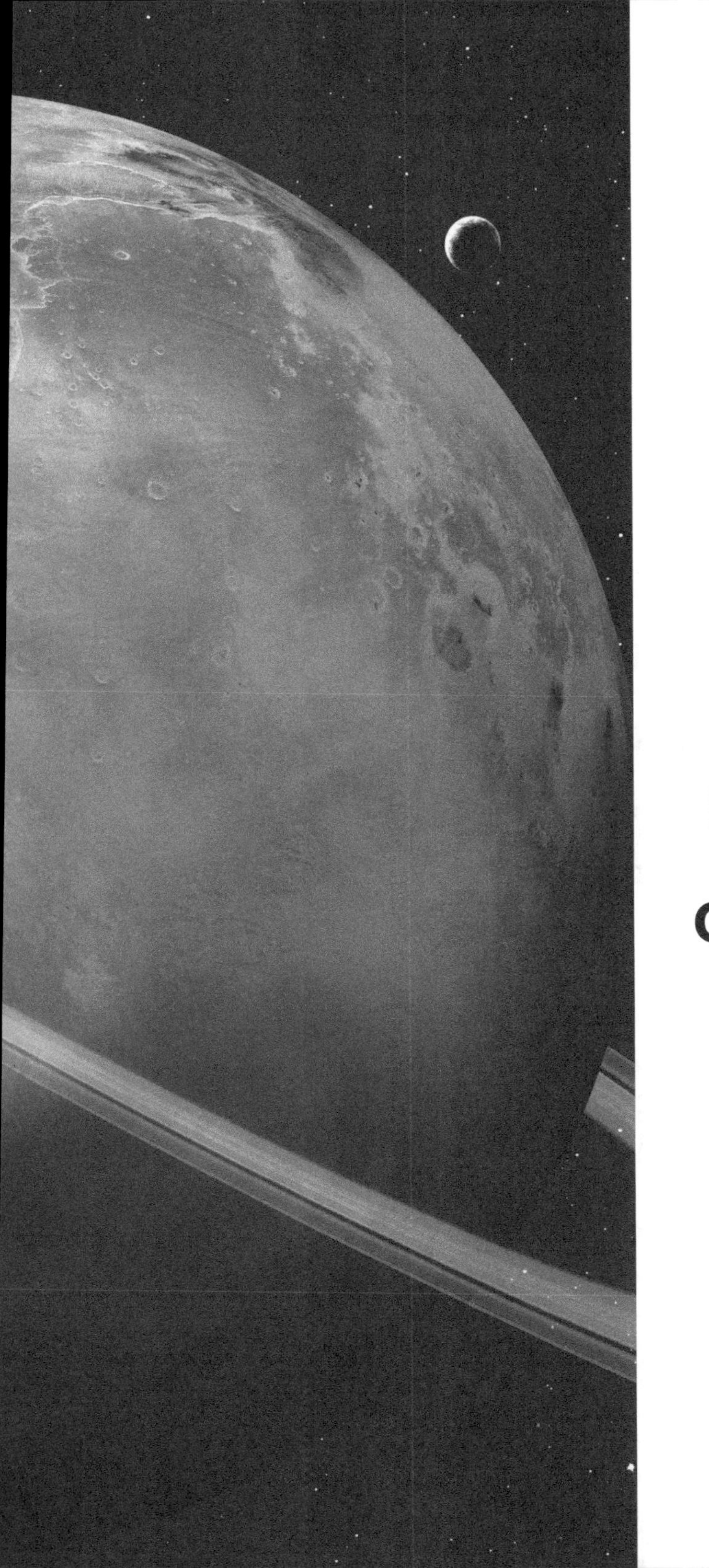

It takes 17.9
hours for
Uranus to turn
on its own axis.

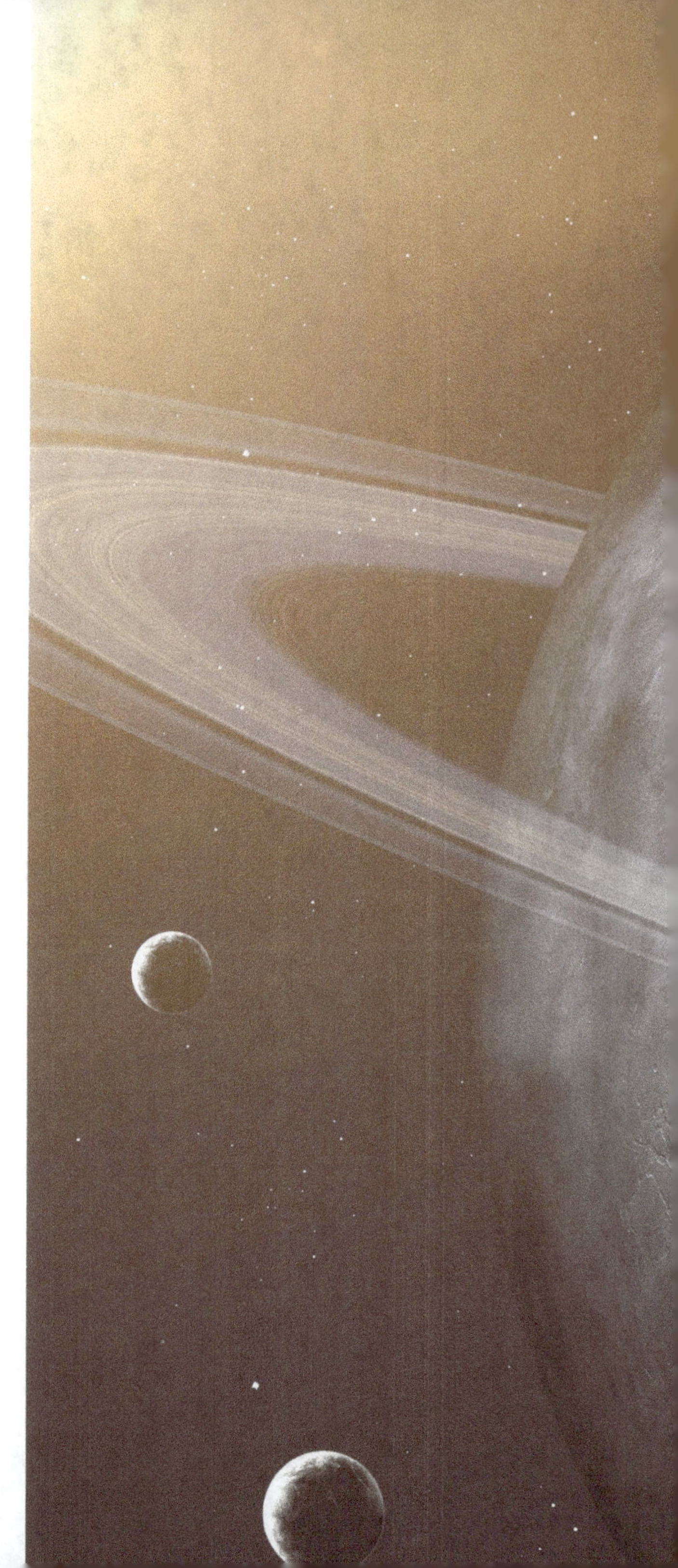

Uranus was named after the ancient Greek God of the heavens.

Uranus is
the smallest
of the four
giant planets.

Uranus is
1,782 million
miles away
from the sun.

The planet has eleven very faint rings.

Scientists have not yet discovered exactly what causes those rings or what they are made of.

Uranus' temperature is almost always the same.

Research
and learn
more about
the planet
URANUS!
Have fun!

Visit
BABY PROFESSOR
EDUCATION KIDS
www.BabyProfessorBooks.com
to download Free Baby Professor eBooks
and view our catalog of new and exciting
Children's Books